The Gates of the Kingdom

Part 2

by Colin Russell Baker

....

Published by Kingdomgates Publishing in the Northern Territory of Australia. **www.kingdomgatespublishing.com.au** Copyright © 2012 Colin Baker.

....

ISBN 10: 1922223980

ISBN 13: 978-1-922223-98-2

Published in Australia

Colin in the Spirit

Dedicated to the Great King,

our glorious Lord and Savior,

Yeshua the Messiah; Adonai

Kabod; the Lord of Glory.

❉ ❉ ❉ ❉ ❉

Contents

'The Gates of the Kingdom' is a book series which will take you on a spiritual pilgrimage, exploring events where the realms of Heaven and Earth have touched.

This pilgrimage is through places which will often be foreign to you. The names of people, places, and relationship terms have been preserved in their original language so that you will get a sense of the cross-cultural context of this amazing story.

You will notice that the narrator speaks only in English, and that his paragraphs always appear indented for your convenience.

Some of the characters are a bit rough around the edges, and some speak with strange accents. These are not spelling mistakes. It will be well worth the effort of getting used to 'reading what you see' with these fellas.

A line dividing text indicates a switching of realms.

The Heritage Series consists of four parts…

The Gates of the Kingdom

~

A story of seed-time and harvest, of sprouting and blossoming, of bearing fruit with seed unto the fullness ... A Kingdom sown, a Kingdom reaped, a glorious Bride without spot or wrinkle, a matchless gift from a Father to a Son; bone of His bone and flesh of His flesh.

Heritage Series

Part 2:

Paw-rach! The Rod Sprouts!

Prologue:

And it was the word of Jehovah to me, saying, Jeremiah, what do you see? And I said; I see an almond rod. (paw-rach[1]) *Then Jehovah said to me. You have seen well, for I will watch over My word to perform it. (Jeremiah 1:11-12 LITV)*

...and the Word was with God, and the Word was God. (John 1:1b LITV)

---

1   Paw-rach: An Ancient Hebrew root; almond, watching, vigilant, to burst forth or break out.

And he brought him (Abram) outside and said, Look now at the heavens and count the stars, if you are able to count them. And he said to him, So shall your seed be. And he believed in Jehovah. And he counted it to him for righteousness. (Genesis 15:5-6 LITV)

And he said to Abram, You must surely know that your seed shall be an alien in a land not theirs; and they shall serve them. And they shall afflict them four hundred years; and I also shall judge the nation whom they serve; and afterward they shall come out with great substance.

And you shall come to your fathers in peace. You shall be buried in a good old age. And in the fourth generation they shall come here again; for the iniquity of the Amorites is not yet full. (Genesis 15:13-16 LITV)

In that day Jehovah made a covenant with Abram, saying, I have given this land to your seed, from the river of Egypt to the great river, the Euphrates, the Kenite and the Kenizzite, and the Kadmonite, and the Hittite, and the Perizzite and the Rephaim, and the Amorite, and the Canaanite, and the Girgashite, and the Jebusite. (Genesis 15:18-21 LITV)

Almost eight hundred years have passed by… Melchizedek is gone, Jebus has fallen and the great ash-tree of Mount Moriah is but a stump in the ground. The Amorites have descended into baal worship. Fertility poles to the goddess Ashera display the shame of the people throughout the land. The time is that of the fullness of the sins of the Amorites.

God has remembered His word to Abraham, to Isaac, and to Jacob, and a people – freed ones too numerous to count – have come out from Egypt.

They have tasted the bitter waters of Marah made sweet by Jehovah their healer. They have drunk from the waters of Elim, where twelve springs have produced seventy palm trees. A testimony, an experience with Jehovah is beginning to shape a people ...each seed bearing fruit after its own kind.

They have assembled before desolate Horeb, the mountain of God ...clan by clan; all the armies of the Lord. And clan by clan they have camped in a natural sort of way. Booths, humpies, and makeshift shelters of all kinds cover the landscape as far as the eye can see...

Looking across this vast shantytown of people and goats, sticks and branches, sheep and mules, over toward the mountain, lays the camp of the Kohathites ...Some seventeen thousand or so men, women children and babies, packed into four huge clusters around the booths of Moses, Aaron, Elzaphan and Korah.

The clans of Amran first, then Izhar, Hebron, and Uzziel each in their own cluster…

❊ ❊ ❊ ❊ ❊

The Camp

As the first rays of dawn come flooding across the flatland on the west, the whole scene bursts into life…

People everywhere, streaming out to squat in frosty fields brilliant in the morning light. All gathering something like the frost itself … Everybody carrying something back to camp in sacks, in buckets and in pots.

From all across the camp comes the clatter of pots and pans, of people waking and babies crying.

At the far side towards the mountain a man stands watching and waiting with family members seated all around. Among them two brothers, Nadab and Abihu wait impatiently:

"Why must we always be the last to eat? Nobody else is waiting." complained the younger.

"Don't you know anything?" replied Nadab. "But why should you complain? You always drink when you milk the goats."

Abihu frowns, his bright, dark eyes searching for a reply.

"Look! The milk is still on your whiskers!"

"Well if you took your turn at some of the work around here maybe there'd be milk all over your face!" yelled the younger in a fuming whisper, wiping the corner of his mouth.

Just then, Elisheba appeared with her mornings reward in a sack which she immediately handed to Aaron. Taking the sack in both hands, he lifted it high above his head and gave thanks to Jehovah for the bread of Heaven. All the people bowed and pronounced their agreement.

By the time most had risen, Abihu was up and away with Nadab almost hot on his heels.

"Nadav!" It was Aaron. He stopped and waited for the inevitable.

"Nadav! Come! I want a word with you Ben (Son)."

"It was Avihu, he…"

"'Ahiha (your brother) is under discipline, just as you were at his age."

"But 'Avi (My Father), he…"

"The point is not what he said, but how we shall react. Ben (Son); consider this place. Here we are before the mountain of Y'haveh. With a mighty hand He has brought us here to Himself and we all stand as ben (sons) before Him. Must I remind you of the place of honor that Y'haveh has so graciously given us?"

"Yes 'Av."

"As for Avihu, I think the time has come for him to take some responsibility too for our position in the camp. I'll talk with him also. Both of you must stop your bickering. Do you understand?"

"Yes 'Av (Father), I understand."

"Come then, imha (your mother) will have breakfast ready by now. We shall eat and we shall talk."

After the morning meal people began moving about the camp. Nadab and Abihu went with Elkanah and Abi' to check out the cloud standing before Horeb. Just beyond Moses shelter, they found a clear place where they could see the cloud.

They sat and gazed at it for a long time. There seemed to be a fire inside of it, which occasionally could be seen even in daylight, like a flickering glow deep within the pillar.

They had grown quite accustomed to the presence of the cloud and often had come to gaze at it with awe and wonder...

"Y'haveh must be like fire!" uttered Abihu.

"Yeah!" whispered Abi' and Elkanah in unison. "Absolutely awesome!" added Elkanah. "What do you reckon he's gon'na do now?"

"I don't know," said Nadab, "but 'Avi says that we've come here to worship him."

"Yeah! Awesome; eh!"

"Do you reckon he's watching us?" asked Abi', as he moved a bit closer to his older brother.

"I reckon he knows we're here," answered Nadab, "but I don't think he minds because he loves us. He saved us from Par'oh and brought us here. Besides; don't forget; 'Avi is his Cohen (Priest) and that means we're more special than anyone else in all Isra'el. One day we shall rule with Y'haveh!"

"What about Moshe," asked Elkanah "isn't he our leader?"

"Yeah," replied Nadab, "but don't forget it was Aharon who spoke to Par'oh, and besides his ben are different to us. You know what I mean."

"But 'Ah (Brother), weren't you there when we all ate that fellowship meal together before the Lord? You know, with Yitro, Moshe's hoten (father in law)? Even 'Avi gave him a brother's welcome!"

Suddenly a flash of fiery light from within the cloud sent them all lunging for the cover of a small rock. The ground trembled like rolling thunder and sunlight blazed down on them.

Abi' began to cry. Elkanah grabbed hold of him, covering his mouth with his hand. They all cowered together in a huddle behind that rock for what seemed like ages. Eventually it was Abihu who found the courage to look up towards the mountain. The fiery pillar was gone and the cloud had come down on top of Horeb.

They all leapt up and ran into camp, shouting aloud the news which everyone was already gazing at in bewilderment.

"Elohim[2] is on the Mountain! Elohim is on the mountain!"

Joshua came running across the camp with young Eli', son of Moses, at his side.

They paused briefly at the camp of Aaron where they were joined by Abihu and Eli'ezer. The four of them ran on to ascend a small pile of boulders just beyond the camp of Korah…

Lifting the ram's horn slung about his neck, Joshua sounded the distinctive two-toned blast for meeting, first towards the clan of Merari, then to the Gershonites. He waited, catching his breath, listening for the resound.

He was about to sound another blast when he remembered Eli', who was watching and waiting. Quickly un-slinging the horn, he handed it to Eli', who had instantly jumped to his side. Putting his strong arm around Eli's shoulders, they balanced together there, atop that rather small boulder.

---

2   Elohim: Great One (plural); God.

Eli' let out a blast loud and clear which almost immediately found a response from Zuriel of Merari. He turned and with great enthusiasm sounded the second call to the Gershonites. It was picked up in the camp of Lael. The call to meet began to echo gate to gate across the whole camp.

Young Eli' jumped down to the applause of his brothers. He was about to show off the rams horn when Joshua landed in the middle of them. They all laughed and Joshua took over the showing off of the horn…

"That, my young 'ah, (brothers) is the way we call our elders to a meeting. You must never make that sound unless Moshe gives the command. If you do, you'll be in big trouble."

All the elders made their way to the meeting ground in front of the camp of Aaron, about a hundred and twenty men in all.

Moses raised both hands and silence fell upon the meeting:

"Ben Isra'el, Eloheinu[3] Y'haveh, who has brought us here to himself, has moved. The pillar of cloud is no longer standing before us. Elohim is on Horev."

---

3   Eloheinu: Our God

"This is the place where I first heard his voice. This is the holy mountain of which I spoke, saying; we shall worship Eloheinu before his holy mountain."

"It was here that he appeared to me as a flame of fire in a thorn bush, and the thorn bush was not consumed. Here, he commanded me to remove my sandals for the ground had become holy. This is the place!"

"Now I know that Y'haveh is on the mountain. He waits for me to go up and we wait for his command. Does anyone wish to speak?"

Elzaphan raises his hand; "'Ah (Brothers), Moshe is the only one among us who speaks with Y'haveh. What shall we do if he doesn't come back or is delayed?"

A rumble of agreement resounds around the circle, quickly degenerating into a disorderly gabble of complaint.

Moses raises a hand, waits …and speaks; "'Ah, I hear your concern. Aharon and Hur are with you, and I shall take Y'hoshua with me, but only to the foot of the mountain. You should all wait here with Aharon. If I'm delayed in speaking with Y'haveh, Y'hoshua will return to you with my instructions."

And Moses went up to God. And Jehovah called to him from the mountain, saying. You shall say this to the house of Jacob and tell it to the sons of Isra'el. You have seen what I did to Egypt; and I bore you on wings of eagles and brought you to Me. And now, if you will surely listen to my voice, and will keep My covenant, you shall become a special treasure to Me above all the nations, for all the earth is mine.

And you shall become a kingdom of priests for Me, a holy nation. These are the words which you shall speak to the sons of Isra'el.

('...king of Salem and priest of the most high God.') (Remember the seed?)

And Moses came and called the elders of the people. And he put all these words before them which Jehovah commanded him. And all the people answered together and said; All which Jehovah has spoken we will do. And Moses brought back the words of the people to Jehovah. (Exodus 19:3-8)

The sun was low in the sky and fires were being kindled. Small wisps of smoke and the smell of burning acacia had begun wafting up from all over camp when Eli', Abihu and Gershom came running in with the news; "They're coming! They're coming!"

Aaron himself was standing to greet them.

"Avihu, Come! Where have you been Ben?"

"I was with Gershom and Eli', 'Av. We went only to the edge of the camp."

"That's alright Ben. Make sure you never go beyond the camp near the mountain."

"Yes 'Avi I know, but why?"

"Don't always question me Ben. Is it any wonder that imcha (your mother) and I must forever worry about you; where you are, what you are doing! You should spend more time with Nadav, and you can start by helping him with the water."

"But 'Avi, didn't we fetch water this morning?"

"Ben, I want you to fetch cool water from the rock for Moshe and Y'hoshua."

"Oh! Alright 'Avi," replied Abihu cheerfully as he turned to go.

"Take Nadav with you!" called Aaron, throwing up his hands in mock surrender.

As they approached the rock, the cloud over Horeb, fiery in the setting sun reflected deep red in the shallow sea of water spreading out in all directions. The country was so flat that every salt bush and every small rock protruded from the mirror surface as if some vast flock of birds were feeding in the water.

"Hey 'Ah (Brother), I know a shortcut. Do you want to see?"

"There's too much mud to cross there. It's alright for you to get covered in white clay. Don't forget, we'll have to carry this water into the meeting ground when we get back!"

"Yeah; I know, but there are rocks. We can jump from one to another."

"You can jump. I'm going round!"

There was a long, narrow ridge of desert sand, formed by a thousand windstorms trailing out from behind the rock. Nadab struck out for the far end of the bar, but Abihu wandered out into ankle deep water.

It was only fifty meters or so across to dry ground, but the light was fading fast.

'Now here's the deep mud, but,' he questioned to himself with an element of panic, 'where is that rock? Oh yeah, I remember; the stick …near the stick. Yeah … There it is.'

Taking a broad step he began picking his way from rock to rock across the fiery mirror, sending ripples in all directions as he went. Reaching the other side just a little ahead of Nadab, he sat down on the sandy ridge to wait.

From out of the mountain ravine, a flock of birds came low across the water. They were flying straight-line towards Abihu when suddenly they turned in perfect unison, and went back. It was Nadab. They had seen him.

Abihu heard his footsteps and looked up.

"Took your time, didn't you!"

Nadab stopped and caught his breath.

"Well, come on then, there's no time for sitting around. They'll be wanting this water by now. Where've you been all day anyway?"

Abihu ignored the question.

"Hey! Look at those birds!" He exclaimed; "They're landing on the rock!"

"Well, they won't be there for long. Come on. Let's go."

They both set off at a faster pace, their approach triggering a great whirring of wings to the cry of a thousand birds spiraling up into the heavens above, not willing to part fully with the treasure they had found.

They both reached the rock together. Cool, clean water was gushing out from its brokenness. It flooded out across the sand of a scorched desert clay pan that had so recently been the very epitome of lifelessness and despair.

Abihu climbed up and his brother handed him both skins.

"Don't drop the corks!" He shouted over the roar of gushing waters and the screeching of startled birds.

Lying flat atop the great rock, he reached down into the gaping crevice. Filling both skins, he tossed them down to Nadab. Mission accomplished, they hurried back through the encroaching darkness.

And I do not want you to be ignorant brothers, that our fathers were all under the cloud; and all passed through the sea, and all ate the same spiritual food. And all drank the same spiritual drink; for they drank of the spiritual rock following — and that rock was Christ. (1 Corinthians 10:1-4 LITV)

✽ ✽ ✽ ✽ ✽

The Gates of the Kingdom

~

A story of seed-time and harvest, of sprouting and blossoming, of bearing fruit with seed unto the fullness ... A Kingdom sown, a Kingdom reaped, a glorious Bride without spot or wrinkle, a matchless gift from a Father to a Son; bone of His bone and flesh of His flesh.

Heritage Series

The Gate in the Camp

"Ah ...that was wonderful! Thank you Dod, (Beloved relative) there's no water like this water. Praise be to Adonai! Fresh and clear like the One who gave it."

"'Ah (brothers), I carried your words to Y'haveh. He had already received them. This is what he commanded: Today and tomorrow, we must separate all of Isra'el to Eloheinu (our God). All the people must wash themselves and their garments and be ready for the third day."

"On the third day, Y'haveh will come down on the mountain before the eyes of all the people!"

Excitement and trepidation ran wild around the circle as men jumped to their feet, embracing, hitting one another and hollering. They totally forgot they were elders. Those that were too old to jump and holler, just stood and grinned at those who did, some edging backwards to save being bowled over in the excitement.

Eventually Joshua sounded his horn at Moses command and sanity returned to the gray haired 'children' of Israel.

"We are to set limits to the mountain all around. None of the people may go up the mountain. Each of you who are here tonight should warn his people. Is there anyone missing? …No?"

"Y'hoshua, my right hand, you shall post sentries about the mountain. Anyone touching the mountain shall be killed …He shall not live, whether man or beast."

"Amen! Amen!" echoed spontaneously around the circle.

They were all so excited, they would have 'amened' just about anything.

"Today and tomorrow we must prepare. Every man shall keep fully devoted to Adonai. Let no man go near a woman."

That sobered them!

"'Ah Aharon, we must sanctify all the people in just two days. We will need a lot of help."

"Zikhri, Korach, Nefeg, Misha'el, Eltzafan; come with us now and bring your elder ben with you. We must find a way to do this."

With that the meeting dispersed…

✳ ✳ ✳ ✳ ✳

"Nadav ! Avihu ! Come my ben, the time has come for both of you to take your place with your elders. There are duties to be performed. Come with me and listen carefully."

We all followed behind Moshe and Father, falling into single file as we wound our way through the crowded camp to a blazing fire in front of Moshe's lean-to. There were about thirty of us I s'pose.

Gershom and Eli' were still throwin' branches on the fire when we all arrived. Moshe himself carried over two heavy rolls of hemp-cloth, which Auntie Tzip' and our cousins quickly helped him to roll out for us guests. 'Very different to our place,' I thought.

We were all a pretty scraggly bunch sitting around the fire that night. We'd been over two months in the desert and most of us had never even thought of having a wash, until tonight that is.

Nadav and I sat beside Father, I on the left and Nadav on the right. We all huddled pretty close together to get onto the cloth. Because we were with Father, we got to sit upwind of the fire. For a while we all just sat there waiting. The old people were all talking and we just looked at each other with big grins on our faces.

When Moshe sat down things just went quiet and the meeting began. It was Eltzafan's younger brother, Misha'el, who spoke first:

"'Ah (Brothers)," he says, "I think it's about time we all took a bath."

Everyone just cracked up; well, almost everyone. Nadav didn't laugh but I couldn't help myself until I felt Father's hand rest between my shoulders.

Moshe, with a grin from ear to ear held up his hand, "I'm afraid our task is a bit more difficult than that," he says, still with a smile on his face, "All of Isra'el needs to take a bath and wash their clothes, but that's the easy part. If we're to do what Elohim has commanded, then all of us here will have to work very hard to get all of Isra'el to work very hard for the next two days to get ready."

"Washing is important but there are many things to be taken care of. 'Ah, tonight, 'give glory to Adonai' (let's make honest confession tonight); as a people we're in a mess. We must keep that grace which delivered us from bondage."

"Arrogance would be foolish. We must not confront God's holiness with blatant evidence of contentment with our dilapidated state. Under the circumstances, this would constitute rebellion. If we did this, we would be consumed. Y'haveh would burst forth on us like fire. This is something He does not want to happen. Surely Y'haveh's people must show a desire to be like the One they follow."

"Not only must we be clean, but there must be no fighting, no angry looks, and definitely no whiskey," he says, looking at Uncle Zith who immediately bowed his baldy head, putting the grins back on quite a few faces around the circle.

"Let all Isra'el devote themselves fully to Y'haveh today and tomorrow. The next day, we shall all meet Eloheinu (our God)."

"Tell this to all the people!"

"When the horn to assemble is heard, everyone, from the oldest to the youngest shall come leaving all things in the camp. Whoever has any matter against his 'ah or against her 'ahot (sister) shall lay it aside. These days are set apart to Y'haveh. It is a holy convocation not only to Y'haveh Eloheinu, but with Y'haveh himself!"

"Tell this to all the people!"

"The head of each clan must take responsibility for his own clan. You my ben shall visit each and every one."

"Decide now how you shall do this. I'll wait for your answer."

It seemed to take forever for our elders to settle the matter. We just watched and waited … Moshe also. I liked Uncle Moshe very much. He was a very patient and gentle man …most of the time.

They finally reached an agreement and Father presented a long list of who would go where.

Nadav and I were to go to Y'huda, to the camp of Uncle Nachshon first. He's our mother's brother.

The next morning, as we came near the camp, our cousin Salmon came out to meet us; a wiry desert runt with curly, raven hair. He was much shorter than me and a whole lot younger too.

"Come, Ben Dod, 'Avi's been waiting for you. What's going on?"

"Big news!" replied Nadav, stirring even more our cousin's vibrant curiosity.

"What?!"

"You'll see."

We rounded the side of one very long lean-to, which was mostly black goat-hair cloth with only a few gaps being filled by old garments.

Uncle Nachshon was sitting in the shelter of this patchwork wall along with half a dozen other elders whom neither of us recognized. He rose up to greet us … something of a new experience to me, and kissed us both in the custom of our people.

Wow! A brother's welcome from Uncle!

"Come!"

We went and sat down in the gate amongst the chiefs of Peretz!

Anticipation and very great excitement took hold of the whole camp in those days.

At the rising of the morning star on the third day, Moshe and Father and all us young men of K'hat met together around the biggest collection of double handled water jars and hyssop branches[4] I've ever seen.

"'Ahi , this is the day." I felt so proud of Father when he spoke from his honored place. "You shall take your stand today in a line across the whole western boundary of the camp …Two of you to each vessel."

---

4   Hyssop branches; Used for sprinkling because of the tendency of the leaves to hold water.

"When the people come through to meet Y'haveh, you shall sanctify them with water from the rock and you shall cry out 'Holy to Adonai!'"

As he spoke this command, Father dipped his hyssop into the water and waved it over all of us many times: "Holy to Adonai! …Holy to Adonai! …Holy to Adonai!"

As the water hit me, I felt a strange sensation that I suspect came over all of us. We didn't really know what it was, but somehow we felt different; kind of new. Our manner changed and we set about our task without our old shyness and fear.

It seemed like some of us became men that morning.

As the day dawned, there came the sound of rolling thunder. There was lightning and heavy cloud on the mountain. We began to realize that we really were in the middle of something very awesome.

Suddenly there came the sound of a ram's horn. It was so loud. Our strength melted away at the very sound of it.

Moshe came out from the camp and all the people followed behind him. When he reached us, he stopped and faced the people, motioning them to come through.

We were all afraid, but when Moshe went through our line, the people followed.

As they came through, we dipped the hyssop and flung that water far and wide, shouting 'Holy to Adonai!' We could hardly hear ourselves because of the horn of Y'haveh and soon became dripping wet. I vividly remember Shimai walking up to me with his hands raised and shouting, 'Drench me! I will die holy!'

We sanctified over two million people that day.

When the last of the people had gone through, we dropped the hyssop and followed behind them. We could feel a rumbling in the ground as we went.

Y'haveh came down on the mountain in fire and Horev started smoking like a furnace.

The whole mountain was shaking and it was difficult to stand. Our knees had turned to jelly and the people all clung together because we were too frightened to fall over. Horev was true to its name that day.

Nadav and I with Gershom and Eli' began pushing our way through. We wanted to see what was happening up front in the gate where Moshe and Father were. We didn't realize that all our wet brothers were following behind us.

As we got almost to the front we could see the spears of Y'hoshua's men and we could see Moshe walking up the lower slope. He stopped and with his hands cupped to his mouth, called out 'Y'haave-hh!' …and he answered him …and we heard the sound of his voice!

And Jehovah came down on the mountain of Sinai, to the top of the mountain, and Moses went up.

And Jehovah said to Moses; Go down, warn the people, lest they break through to gaze at Jehovah, and many of them fall.

And also the priests, those approaching Jehovah, let them sanctify themselves that Jehovah not burst forth among them.

And Moses said to Jehovah. The people are not able to come up to the mountain of Sinai. For You warned us, saying, Set limits to the mountain and sanctify it.

And Jehovah said to him, Come, go down. And you come up and Aaron with you. And let not the priests and the people break through to come up to Jehovah, lest He burst forth among them.

And they said to Moses, You speak with us and we will hear. And let us not speak with God, that we not die.

And Moses said to the people, Do not be afraid, for God has come in order to test you, and so that His fear may be on your faces, that you may not sin.

And the people stood from a distance, and Moses went near the thick darkness where God was. (Exodus 19:20-25 / 20:19-21 LITV)

And Y'haveh Elohim gave to Moshe all the commands and judgments that were on his heart to give for us. And it was like he knew us. He knew us better than we knew ourselves. And he commanded us like we were his own sons.

And He said to Moses, Come up to Jehovah, you and Aaron, Nadab and Abihu, and seventy from the elders of Isra'el. And bow yourselves from a distance. And let Moses approach by himself to Jehovah, and they shall not approach. And the people shall not go up with him.

And Moses came and told all the words of Jehovah to the people, and all the judgments. And all the people answered with one voice and said; We will do all the words which Jehovah has spoken.

The place went quiet. Moshe turned and bowed low to Adonai. All the people did the same, and we worshiped, and we went back to camp.

That evening no-one was allowed into the camp of Moshe. We could see him sitting near the fire till late into the night, working on a roll of parchment. He was writing. None of us were interested in sleep that night. In the gate of every camp, the people sat around their fires most of the night, talking.

And Moses rose early in the morning and built an altar below the mountain and twelve memorial pillars for the twelve tribes of Israel.

And he sent young men of the sons of Israel. And they offered up burnt offerings, and offered sacrifices of bullocks, peace offerings to Jehovah.

And Moses took half of the blood, and put it in basins. And he sprinkled half of the blood on the altar.

And he took the book of the covenant, and read in the ears of the people. And they said; We will do all that Jehovah has spoken, and we will hear.

And Moses took the blood and sprinkled on the people, and said; Behold the blood of the covenant which Jehovah has cut with you concerning these words.

Something had changed.

We were still the same, except that we all had spots of invisible blood in our hair, on our faces and on our clothes. But at that momentous moment we felt a new relationship with our God and with each other. We sensed a fellowship in the sprinkling; a fellowship of blood. This to me seemed unimaginable because we were already one blood, or so one would think!?

Everything old seemed so insignificant, and there was a very great sense of hope welling up inside of us.

❋ ❋ ❋ ❋ ❋

For me and Nadav, it seemed that those days had all been an incredible climb but this day would transcend all of our wildest dreams …and it was real!

Moshe and Father took the lead, and we followed very close behind them with the seventy following behind us. Horev was steep and it wasn't easy for some of the older ones to keep up with us, but when we began to enter the cloud, everyone seemed to bunch up together very quickly.

We spoke only in whispers…

"Nadav."

"What?"

"Some-thing's worrying me."

"What?"

"He called us by name. I mean you and me. Why do you reckon he did that?"

"I already told you, I don't know. I reckon it's got something to do with 'Av."

"Do you think he's planning to give us a special place in Levi?"

"'Ah… I think he already has."

As we wound our way around the central peak, we were forced into single file. Y'haveh was very quiet …so were we. He must have known that our hearts were pounding. Maybe He could hear them. I reckon old Uncle Eltzafan would have died standing if there'd been any rumbling like the day before.

We just started to clear the cloud when we reached the summit. There were pillars of cloud billowing up all around. We appeared to be alone, but it sure didn't feel like we were.

It seemed to me like we had climbed into Heaven itself. I had never before looked out on the tops of the clouds neither did I know anyone who had. There seemed to be a lot more light than normal. Then we realized that we all had two shadows.

We all turned about to see this huge pillar of cloud glowing brilliantly on the west. It swirled around to the north and there he was! Standing there! He was the source of the light! Under his feet was like a shiny pavement of sapphire, clear as the sky itself.

We stood atop Horev like on a great rock in a sea of clear polished sapphire with Y'haveh enthroned upon the sea.

We all bowed down and worshiped him and we lived! We were all amazed that we didn't die.

I thought I heard a gentle voice calling me. I looked up, and we all looked up together.

There was a table of purest gold set with plates and cups. There was bread and there was wine. We ate and we drank and we saw God and we lived.

Behold, I stand at the door and knock; If anyone hears my voice and opens the door, I will go in to him, and I will dine with him and he with Me. (Revelation 3:20 LITV)

I don't remember climbing down that mountain, but apparently, we did.

❋ ❋ ❋ ❋ ❋

The Gates of the Kingdom

~

A story of seed-time and harvest, of sprouting and blossoming, of bearing fruit with seed unto the fullness... A Kingdom sown, a Kingdom reaped, a glorious Bride without spot or wrinkle, a matchless gift from a Father to a Son; bone of His bone and flesh of His flesh.

Heritage Series

The Testing

And Jehovah said to Moses, Come up to Me to the mountain, and be there. (Exodus 24:12a LITV)

And Moses came into the midst of the cloud, and he went up into the mountain. And Moses was in the mountain forty days and forty nights. (Exodus 24:18 LITV)

And Jehovah spoke to Moses of making a sanctuary so that He could dwell with them. He spoke of an ark for the testimony of Israel and of a covering for it of mercy and grace. He spoke of golden images; of spiritual beings ... hammered out of one piece of fine gold with the mercy seat.

These would form a place of symbol where man and God would meet.

He spoke to him of a golden table with plates and cups and pitchers; a table for the bread of His presence; for the bread of those who hunger for His face ...of the lamp-stand of 'Jirah'; the One who sees, who has provided and is Himself 'Our Provision' ...the lamp-stand of the One who watches over His Word to bring it to fullness: Paw-rach! All covered in almond buds and blossoms!

He spoke of the sanctuary of curtains, each curtain joined to her sister to form one 'heavenly' dwelling place.

He spoke of the altar and the courtyard. Then of Aaron, He said these words:

And you shall take to yourself your brother Aaron, and his sons with him, from among the sons of Israel, for him to serve as priest to me; Aaron, Nadab, Abihu, Eliazar and Ithamar, the sons of Aaron. And you shall make holy garments for your brother Aaron, for glory and for beauty; to sanctify him for his serving as priest to Me. (Exodus 28:1-2,3b LITV)

He went on to instruct Moses in the setting apart of the priests and in all the laws of the offerings. These would speak to Heaven and earth by token of the costliness of God's grace.

And He spoke of a small golden altar from which incense would waft heavenward like the prayers of His children:

And you shall put it in front of the veil which is beside the ark of the testimony, there where I meet with you.

And Aaron shall burn incense of perfume on it morning by morning, when he dresses the lamps he shall burn it. And when he sets up the lamps between the evenings, he shall burn it, a perpetual incense before the face of Jehovah for your generations.

You shall not offer up strange incense on it, and burnt offering and food offering; and you shall not pour out drink offering to go up on it. And Aaron shall make atonement on its horns once a year, from the blood of the sin offering of the atonement, once a year he shall make atonement on it for your generations; it is most holy to Jehovah. (Exodus 30:6-10 LITV)

For Moses, those forty days passed so quickly being fully consumed with his Lord and Master. In the camp, the story was very different.

The first few weeks seemed to be relatively uneventful. Certainly they were in contrast to the experience on the mountain. Most families spent their time making and trading for tents. All the animals were shorn whether goats, camels or sheep. Even the poles which they had collected along the way of the sea were being put to better use.

For Nadab and Abihu, it seemed that the descent from the mountain had not ended when they got back to camp. Moses and Joshua were not there and the camp of Aaron had become the meeting ground for all Israel. This meant chores. Chores on top of chores, and their father had no time for them at all. The evening meal was becoming a wearisome thing either focused on every-ones problems or on forgetting every-ones problems...

"Nadav: Go and tell 'aviha[5] that dinner's ready."

"I already did 'Em."

"Well tell him again, he's forgotten."

"I'll go," offered Abihu, knowing the reason for his brother's reluctance. He tossed aside the rope he had been splicing and stepped out into the encroaching darkness.

The two of them had grown very close during those days, and in an ordinary kind of way, taken charge over the affairs of their own camp. Especially over their two younger brothers, Eli'ezer and Ithamar, who now fetched the water, milked the goats and gathered the firewood.

---

5   'aviha: your father

Abihu noticed that most of the onlookers had already left the 'gate', which was where the family had in the past, always eaten meals together. The sun had long set, yet there was no fire…

I knew that there was trouble between the M'rari and the K'nizi. They'd been pledging their daughters to each other, but an old, unresolved breach of vows had capitulated into payback on both sides. Each claimed that the other was the debtor.

It had been brought to Father because the brothers of the rejected bride had been fighting with their cousins. They all kept goats, and had begun slinging stones at each other. One of our young cousins had got hurt …bad.

I always knew those K'nizi were a hot-headed bunch, but this was ridiculous. They'd been talking for hours, and they were still glaring at each other across the circle …and cursing.

Father saw me waiting and motioned for me to come closer.

"Tell imha that I will be late Ben. Don't wait for me. Nadav may give thanks and you may pronounce the blessing."

That was all he had time to say. These people weren't going home without a settlement.

I went back to our shelter. I just shook my head. We all knew that Father wouldn't be coming.

After the meal, Nadav and I went to see Gershom and Eli' to find out whether any of Hur's men had brought a report from Y'hoshua. But, as always, there was none.

I remember well the look in Father's eyes that night. He was waiting anxiously by the fire, and had not yet eaten. When he saw us, that we had no news, he just buried his face in his hands and shook his head. We left them alone and unrolled our bedding.

We could hear them talking late into the night. Me n' Nadav just lay there looking up at the stars. They were so bright it seemed like you could just reach out and touch them.

It seemed so strange to me. Here we were in the desert, months from anywhere, and we were still fighting and arguing with each other.

"'Ah."

"What?"

"Things seem to be piling up on 'Avinu. I'm worried."

"Yeah, so am I. 'Avinu will find a way. We really only need to hold out a bit longer anyway … Moshe should be back soon."

"I hope you're right. I think we almost had a clan war break out today, and I'll bet they're still not satisfied. Can you believe those K'nizi? Little Zuri was the one with the blood all over his face, and they reckon they've been cheated!"

"I heard he got hit in the eye."

"No, but almost. It looked like it, but it split open his eyebrow. I saw it myself at Dod Livni's. That's where they were patching him up."

"What were you doing there?"

"'Av sent me. He wants the K'hat to meet in the morning. I guess he's calling for help."

"Yeah, we sure need it, but no-one's gon'na come to any meeting while this is going on."

"Yeah, we're still the same aren't we."

"Well they might be, but we're not still the same. We're not slaves any more, are we?"

"No, but the people are still fighting and blaming one another for everything. I reckon they'll be blaming us if this trouble goes any further."

The next morning, while we were still eating breakfast, a bunch of tough K'nizi boys came around. They wanted to know when Moshe would be back. I guess it was their way of saying that they weren't satisfied with Father's decision.

It looked like they were ready for a fight. Nadav and I stood up and our big Egyptian servant, Faiyuk, threw aside the firewood he was carrying. It looked like this was it!

Father stood to his feet, but none of them, or us, were ready for Auntie Miryam.

She came in and let fly. She just tore strips off them with her tongue and then laid into them with a broom! I almost felt sorry for them. They didn't know what to do! They had obviously never encountered anyone like Auntie Miryam before!

By the time we tried to restrain her, all we could do was stop her chasing after them by taking the broom.

That was the only time I saw Father smile in those days...

"Nadav, Avihu, we have a problem. Otni'el is way out of line, and this could so easily spread right through the camp."

I could see that Father was choosing his words carefully. He always appeared so wise to us.

"I cannot ask Hur to discipline his own dod, and it would be very awkward for him to even talk to his 'av about this. Since the death of Hur's saba[6], Y'funeh, Kalev has been the only one with any influence on Otni'el. Kalev is a good man."

"I want you both to go to Kalev and tell him what has happened here this morning. Perhaps he might be able to stop this discontent from spreading any further."

"Don't worry 'Avi," I said, "I've been to the camp of Kalev many times with Y'hoshua and Gershom. We'll speak with him. Everything will be alright."

But everything was not 'alright'. Nadav and I both knew that the K'nizi boys did whatever they liked, and it was pretty much the same throughout the camp with our generation.

To make matters worse, Uncle Zith was back in business again, and doin' a roarin' trade with his 'wine', which you couldn't really call whiskey even, but all us young men were into it. His tents were lookin' real good.

During the week that followed the unrest in the camp just got worse every day. Hur had called his armed men back from their duty at the foot of the mountain and stationed them around our camp and his. In their new posts, they needed shields as

---

6   saba: grandfather

well as spears. More and more people came every day. They wanted out of there, and they wanted it bad.

Then one morning, nobody came at all. Things were suddenly quiet. There was a real sense of foreboding in the air. Even the desert breeze off the mountain had stopped…

"What's going on?" I asked Father.

"I don't know Ben." That's when I really started to worry.

Just then, Hur showed up.

"There's a meeting of elders on the other side of camp, and everybody's over there. I expect they'll all be coming this way soon. What shall I tell the men?"

"Tell them to lay aside their spears. We shall listen to what the people have to say."

"Nadav and Avihu, take imha and 'ahinu[7], go to the camp of your Dod Nachshon until this is over. Hur will send some men with you."

And the people saw that Moses delayed to come down from the mountain. And the people gathered to Aaron. And they said to him, Rise up, make for us gods who may go before our face. As for this

---

7   'ahinu: your brothers

Moses, the man who brought us up from the land of Egypt, we do not know what has become of him.

And Aaron said to them, Tear off the rings of gold which are in the ears of your wives, your sons and your daughters; and bring them to me.

And all the people tore off the rings of gold which were in their ears, and brought to Aaron.

And he took from their hand and formed it with an engraving tool. And he made it a casted calf. And they said; These are your gods o' Israel, who made you go up from the land of Egypt. (Exodus 32:1-4 LITV)

And Aaron, looking at the calf, called his sons and servants...

"Nadav, take with you 'ahinu and the 'eved (servants), go quickly and bring rocks and build an altar. Tomorrow we shall celebrate. It shall be a feast to Y'haveh. Everyone will be happy."

And so we did; early the next morning, every-one came. We slaughtered sheep and cattle, we offered up burnt offerings and brought near peace offerings and we ate and we drank and we drank some more and we danced with tambourines and drums and cymbals. We sung again the songs of Egypt.

It seemed that all the people really wanted were mute gods that they could feast their eyes upon. This seemed to make them outrageously happy.

The people went wild and many stripped off their clothes and danced naked before the golden calf as was the custom of reveling in Misrayim.

And Jehovah spoke to Moses, Come, go down, for your people whom you caused to go up from Egypt are corrupted; they have quickly turned off from the way which I commanded them; they have made for themselves a casted calf and have bowed to it. And they have said; These are your gods, o' Israel, who made you go up from the land of Egypt.

And Jehovah said to Moses; I have seen this people and behold it is a stiff-necked people. And now, leave Me alone, that My anger may glow against them, that I may consume them. And I will make you a great nation.

And Moses prayed before the face of Jehovah his God, and said, Why, o' Jehovah, does your anger glow against Your people, whom You caused to go up from the land of Egypt with great power and with a mighty hand.

Why should the Egyptians say, saying, for evil He has caused them to go up, to kill them in the mountains, and to consume them on the face of the earth?

Turn from Your fierce anger and change Your purpose as to the evil to Your people.

Recall Abraham, Isaac and Israel Your servants, to whom You swore by Yourself, and You spoke to them, I will multiply your seed like the stars of the heavens, and all this land which I have said, I will give to your seed. And they shall possess it forever.

And Jehovah changed His purpose concerning the evil which He had spoken to do to His people. (Exodus 32:7-14 LITV)

Moses turned, and with the burden of God's hurt weighing heavy on his heart, went down. The two tablets of the testimony, like a marriage agreement, were in his hand. The tablets were the work of God. The writing was the writing of God.

As Moses and Joshua came near the camp they heard noises and shouting…

"Adoni! …A sound of battle in the camp!"

"No my ben, it's neither the sound of victory nor the cry of defeat. It's the sound of 'ahna; the singing of slaves."

And it happened, as he came near the camp and saw the calf and the dances, the anger of Moses glowed. And he threw the tablets from his hands, and he broke them below the mountain.

And he took the calf, which they had made and burned it with fire, and he ground it until it was fine, then he scattered it on the face of the water. And he made the sons of Israel to drink it. (Exodus 32:19-20 LITV)

As we drank that water, we all knew our guilt. It was a horrevl feeling. It was a part of our experience of Horev.

When Moshe saw the state of the camp; that everyone was just doing whatever they felt like to do; that the men of every clan had no regard for each other… Nadav and I; we couldn't look him in the face.

He went and stood in the old meeting ground, we called it 'the gate', and called out, 'Who is for Adonai? Come to me!'

The whole tribe of Levi went over to Moshe. I guess we were feeling a bit more guilty than anyone else, or at least, I was.

And he said to them, So says Jehovah, God of Israel, each one put his sword on his thigh; pass over to and fro from gate to gate (clan to clan) in the camp, and each one kill his brother, and each his kindred. (Exodus 32:27 LITV)

And we went, and did it, just as Moshe had said! We killed three thousand of our own people in the camp that day! Most of all we killed ourselves. When it was over, I really didn't know who I was any more.

We went back to Moshe all covered in blood. We had nowhere else to go.

Moshe never flinched. Instead, he exhorted us to give ourselves fully to the service of Eloheinu, saying, *"Fill your hand today for Y'haveh, since each one has laid aside his kinship and has become estranged from his ben and from his 'ah to give you a blessing today."*

That which has been, will be. (Ecclesiastes 1:9 LITV)

'We cannot harvest that which has not been sown.'

A stone was cut out of the mountain, but not by human hands. (Daniel 2:45 LITV)

❊ ❊ ❊ ❊ ❊

The Gates of the Kingdom

~

*A story of seed-time and harvest, of sprouting
and blossoming, of bearing fruit with seed
unto the fullness ... A Kingdom sown, a Kingdom reaped, a glorious Bride without spot or
wrinkle, a matchless gift from a Father to a
Son; bone of His bone and flesh of His flesh.*

Heritage Series

The Tent Outside

When the reality of what had happened really set in, it was then that we heard that Y'haveh had said to Moshe, 'Leave! You and the people you brought up from the land of Egypt.' He said that we should move on from Horev and that he would send an angel ahead of us to drive out the people of the land he'd promised us.

He also said he wouldn't be coming.

When we heard this bad news, our hearts sank. We all went into mourning. Everyone stripped off their ornaments, even from their donkeys and camels and tents.

We laid aside everything to wait and see what Y'haveh would do. We were like a pledged bride who had hurt her precious groom. The marriage was off!

Moshe took the tent that Gershom and Eli' had prepared for his return and pitched it far outside the camp.

When I saw them carrying the new tent out, I thought that Moshe was leaving us too. It was too much for us to take. We weren't the only ones, but it was worse for us. Abi' was drowning his sorrows in Uncle Zith's whiskey. We decided to join him.

The next day we woke late. The sun was high and we were half cooked. I had a terrible headache, and couldn't even look at food. Nadav just laughed at me. He seemed to be alright but he didn't eat either, which meant that we began the day with a roasting from Mother about wasting breakfast. Getting sober sure wasn't much fun!

I noticed that Nadav still had the last half skin tucked inside his tunic. He saw my glance, and patted his pocket as if to ask if I wanted some. I shook my head and then wished that I hadn't. He took off somewhere, and I went looking for Eli'.

Eli' and I went to the rock. I needed cool water real bad.

"What happened to you?" he says in a cheery tone that made me feel like I was even more than half dead.

"I was poisoned by Dod Zith. Me and Abi' and Nadav, we were all poisoned."

"You mean you all got drunk?"

"Yeah; I guess that's what happened. I thought you and Gershom were leaving us with Moshe and Doda Tzipp'."

"Leaving! ... Like; to go where?"

"I saw you carrying that tent out yesterday."

"Oh! Where've you been man? That wasn't yesterday. That was the day before! And the tent, it's not for us, it's for Y'haveh!"

"What? I don't understand!"

"It's for him; for Y'haveh. He really does want to come and live with us, but we don't... we aren't... we're not... ah... the desire; it's not mutual. I think we've hurt his feelings."

We'd just begun crossing that sandy ridge, when a thousand startled birds sent shock waves through my head. I couldn't think straight until we reached the water and I'd plunged my head into it.

We sat a while in the shadow of the rock.

"'Avi calls it the tent of meeting. Anyone can go out there to inquire of Adonai. I watched him go out yesterday evening. When he went in, the pillar of cloud came down and stood at the entrance. Everyone bowed down and worshiped.'"

"Has anyone else been into the tent?"

"Yes; Y'hoshua. He went in, and so far he's not come back out."

"Gee, that's strange. I mean Y'hoshua and Y'haveh being outside the camp. It's shameful. We are the ones who have done shamefully; us; the whole house of Isra'el. I don't understand. Why should they be outside the camp?"

Therefore, let us go out to Him who is outside the camp and share his disgrace. For we have no permanent city here; on the contrary, we seek the one to come. (Hebrews 13:13-14 JNT)

And it happened that everyone seeking Jehovah went to the tabernacle of the congregation, which was outside the camp. And it happened as Moses went to the tabernacle the people all rose and stood, each one at the door of his tent. And they looked after Moses until he had gone into the tabernacle.

And Jehovah would speak to Moses face to face as a man speaks to his friend. (Exodus 33:7b-8,11 LITV)

And he (Moses) said, I pray, let me see Your glory. (Let me see Your face.) (Exodus 33:18 LITV)

* * * * *

The Gates of the Kingdom

~

A story of seed-time and harvest, of sprouting and blossoming, of bearing fruit with seed unto the fullness... A Kingdom sown, a Kingdom reaped, a glorious Bride without spot or wrinkle, a matchless gift from a Father to a Son; bone of His bone and flesh of His flesh.

Heritage Series

The Testing II

And Jehovah said to Moses, Cut out for yourself two tablets of stone, like the former. And I will write on the tablets the words which were on the former tablet, which you broke. And be prepared in the morning, and go up in the morning to Mount Sinai. And place yourself by Me on top of the mountain.

And Jehovah came down in the cloud. And he placed himself there with Him, and he called on the name of Jehovah. And Jehovah passed by before his face and called out: Jehovah! Jehovah, God! Merciful and gracious, slow to anger, and great in goodness and truth, keeping mercy for thousands, forgiving iniquity and transgression and sin, and not leaving entirely unpunished, visiting the iniquity of fathers on sons, and on sons of sons, to the third and fourth generation.

And Moses hurried and bowed to the earth and worshiped. And he said, If now I have found favor in Your eyes, O Lord, please let my Lord go in our midst, for it is a stiff-necked people; and You forgive our iniquity and our sin, and take us as a possession.

And He said; Behold I am cutting a covenant; I will do wonderful things before all your people, which not have been done in all the earth and among all nations. And all the people, in whose midst you are, shall see the work of Jehovah, for that which I am about to do is awesome.

And he was there with Jehovah forty days and forty nights; he did not eat bread and he did not drink water. (He laid down his life, for he carried a very vulnerable people upon his heart.) And Jehovah wrote on the tablets the words of the covenant, the Ten Commandments. (Exodus 34:1-2 / 5-10 / 28)

This time things would be different. We all knew when we saw those two empty tablets of stone in Moshe's hand; we were being given a second chance. And things were different! This time we had the tent!

Whenever someone wished to inquire of Adonai, they would go and bow down to the ground some distance from the entrance of the tent.

This was a new thing to us. At first, many people were going just to show their sorrow that we had hurt Y'haveh so. We really did want him to go with us. Then, something really strange began happening.

I noticed that some people seemed to have lots of inquiries to make before Y'haveh. It began to be noticed by everyone because the number of people lying prostrate before the tent seemed to be growing every day. The entrance of the tent outside had become the gate of the whole camp!

There were so many people that the women, eventually thousands of women, began serving in the new gate. They would sit there all day making damper from the manna and serving drinks. The women had always considered this to be their place in the gate. They just kind of naturally came together. This was new yet it seemed like they had been doing it all their lives. An amazing sight! They all actually enjoyed each other's company!

At sunset, Y'hoshua's men would walk through asking the people to go back to camp. They would often be seen stooping down to touch people and gently shake the ones who didn't seem to hear or respond.

Whenever there was an argument, they would often come to Father first. He would send them all together to bow down in the presence of Adonai at the tent. Nobody ever came back to Father.

I saw people rise up out there and apologize to one another without ever having discussed the matter of guilt. We also saw the wives and little ones and the parents of those we had slain going out.

Not many of us from Levi went, but we watched from a distance. I wanted to go, but felt too ashamed. Instead, I would go with Nadav to visit the tents of Uncle Zith. It was the morning after one of these visits that Moshe returned from the mountain.

Father had called a meeting of the K'hat[8] and me and Nadav were late. We knew from the commotion that woke us up that Moshe had returned.

When we arrived at the gate, there were all the elders of K'hat, standing, facing us as we came out of the tent!!

---

8   K'hat: Kohath; Kohathites

At first, I was terrified, thinking they'd been waiting for us! But they had strange looks on their faces! And they weren't even looking at us!

I heard Moshe calling to them from behind and immediately looked over the shoulder of old Uncle Eltzafan to see. There was Moshe, his face shining like an angel! Light, was shining from it!

I was shocked sober! I grabbed hold of Nadav and pointed, but I didn't look. Aharon and all the elders of the people had turned their backs to him. He had become holy from being with Y'haveh! We didn't want to see his face, for his holiness was uncovered.

And Moses spoke to them. And afterwards, all the sons of Israel drew near. And he commanded them to do all which Jehovah had spoken with him in the mountain of Sinai.

And Moses finished speaking with them, and he put a veil on his face. And as Moses came in before Jehovah to speak with Him, he would remove the veil until he went out; and he would go out and speak to the sons of Israel what was commanded.

And the sons of Israel would see the face of Moses; that the skin of the face of Moses had become luminous. And Moses would put the veil back on his face until he went to speak with Him.

And Moses assembled all the congregation of the sons of Israel and said to them, These are the words which Jehovah has commanded to do them: Work may be done six days, and on the seventh day it shall be holy to you, a Sabbath rest to Jehovah;

And Moses said to all the congregation of the sons of Israel, saying, Take from among you an offering to Jehovah.

Everyone willing of heart shall bring it, the offering of Jehovah: Gold and silver and bronze, and blue and purple and crimson and bleached linen, and goats hair, and rams' skins died red, and dugong skins, and acacia wood, and oil for the light, and spices for the oil of anointing, and for the incense of perfumes; and onyx stones, and stones of settings, for the ephod and for the pocket.

And every wise-hearted one of you, let them come and make all which Jehovah has commanded. (Exodus 34:31b-35:2a, 4-10 LITV)

And all the congregation of the sons of Israel rose up from before Moses and went out.

❊ ❊ ❊ ❊ ❊

The Gates of the Kingdom

~

A story of seed-time and harvest, of sprouting and blossoming, of bearing fruit with seed unto the fullness ... A Kingdom sown, a Kingdom reaped, a glorious Bride without spot or wrinkle, a matchless gift from a Father to a Son; bone of His bone and flesh of His flesh.

Heritage Series

The Dwelling Place

Hi! My name is Oholi'av. I know it sounds strange to you. It means 'tent of my father'. His name was Achisamack, which means 'my brother is a support'. He died in Egypt, but I'm here in his place. We're of the sons of Isra'el, of the tribe of Dan.

My father was a tent-maker and also his father before him. I too know how to make tents, but my real skill is in the embroidery of fine linen. I love to work with blue, purple, crimson and bleached fabrics, with gold and with precious stones and with engraving tools.

Avihu asked that I tell you this part of the story of our second chance with Adonai at Horev. It was, for most of us, the best part of the story. He and his brother Nadav were there, but they missed out on many of the wonderful things that happened when we began making the dwelling place for Adonai with its tent and all its furnishings. I think they were very busy with their cousins, the sons of Zithri, much of the time.

Mostly I was working with B'tzal'el, the son of Uri from the tribe of Y'huda. He is the grandson of Hur.

Adonai had mentioned us both by name to Moshe on the mountain and given us charge of all the work! For me, this was the most wonderful thing ever in my whole life. There are many of us who worked together there who'd say the same thing.

When Adonai called for a free-will offering to be brought, all the people were so excited to know that he wasn't leaving us …On the contrary; he was coming to live with us! Wow! You should have seen that offering!

People brought gold, silver, bronze, blue and crimson cloth and yarn as well as bleached linen. They brought rings and belts and all kinds of jewelry, goat hair and ram skins. Lots and lots of acacia wood. Even the dugong skins we'd collected along the way of the sea were brought for the outer covering.

Everyone gave out of a willing heart, not holding anything back.

None of us had known anything like this before.

And the multitude of those who believed, the heart and soul were one. And no one said any of his possessions to be his own, but all things were common to them …and great grace was upon them all … they bore the value of the things that were sold and laid them at the feet of the apostles. (Acts 4:32, 33b, 34b-35 LITV)

Later on Moshe got Avihu's younger brother, Itamar, to make a record of everything that was given. There was over twenty-nine talents (2000lbs) of gold and over one hundred talents (6000lbs) of silver alone.

That was just the beginning, everyone worked with such enthusiasm as I had never seen before, nor ever would see again in all my life.

All the women who were skilled at spinning got to work and spun. All the women whose hearts stirred them to work spun the goat hair.

The leaders brought precious stones. I set them into the breastplate and into the ritual vest for Aharon.

They also brought spices and olive oil for the light, for the anointing oil, and for fragrant incense.

I had some special gold which I had received for my tent-making services in the camp. It was very pure. We hammered it into very thin plates and then cut it into threads which I worked into the ritual vest and breastplate for Aharon.

Each morning, the people would bring more and more. We ran out of places to store it all. Too many of us were kept busy all day just sorting it out. It soon became obvious that we had far more than we needed.

The day came when we had to stop work to go have a meeting with Moshe about the problem. He actually had to command the people to stop giving to the work of Adonai!

Everyone took great pride in the work, especially when each piece was completed. And the quality of the work was exceptionally good. Once a worker was trained, I rarely needed to command that anything be re-done.

Those days were so wonderful that it was easy to lose track of time, especially for me. The shofar[1] of Shavat[2] often took me by surprise.

---

1   shofar: horn
2   Shavat: Sabbath

During the rest of Adonai, we would often sit around talking about the work. There were so many things that just amazed us. It was so exhilarating; just to always find a way to meet the vision …piece by piece.

For me, Shavat was also a time when I could sit quietly and dream. These were the times when Adonai would show me the pattern for all that His servant, Moshe had described to me. It was like ascending out from the Red Sea every time I heard Moshe say 'Yes! That's the way he showed it to me!'

We knew that we were alive and that our lives had purpose! The testimony we shared was wonderful!

As we worked on a dwelling place for Adonai, he was working on a dwelling place for us! It was a part of our experience of Horev. It was right there at Horev that he changed us from being a mob of runaway slaves, into a nation; Isra'el!

There was a great 'birthing' taking place there. Many of us who had vision were awed by it. It could hardly have gone unnoticed, because, as we neared the completion of the Tabernacle, babies began to be born all over the camp … including my own son Natan'el! We had been camped at Horev for over nine months.

In all, the work of the Tabernacle took exactly nine months to complete.

…but You prepared a body (dwelling place) for Me. (Hebrews 10:5b LITV)

And the Word became flesh and tabernacled among us. (John 1:14 LITV)

…and on her head a crown of twelve stars; and having a babe in womb … and she bore a son… (Revelation 12:1b, 2a, 5a LITV)

…the ones … who were … born of God. (John 1:12-13 extracts)

We made the tunics of finely woven linen for Aharon and his sons … Also the turban, the splendid head gear and the shorts, all of finely woven linen. The sash was of blue and scarlet yarn, the work of a weaver in colors.

The work of the ornament of the turban was of pure gold. We engraved upon it the words: 'Holiness to Y'haveh', and tied a blue chord on it to fasten it to the front of the turban as Adonai had ordered Moshe.

And so, all the work for the 'Dwelling Place'; the Tent of Meeting, was finished. We, the people of Isra'el; the whole nation, did all the work, just as Adonai had ordered Moshe. There it was! We had done it! Together; we had done it! Exactly as Adonai had ordered, so we had done. And Moshe blessed us!

And Jehovah spoke to Moses, saying, On the first day of the month, on the first of the month, you shall raise up the tent of the tabernacle of the congregation.

And you shall put there the ark of the testimony, and you shall cover the ark with the veil.

And you shall bring in the table and set in order its arrangement.

And you shall bring in the lamp-stand and set up its lamps.

And you shall put the altar of gold for incense before the ark of testimony.

And you shall set up the hanging of the door of the tabernacle.

And you shall set up the altar of burnt offerings, before the door of the tent of the tabernacle of the congregation.

And you shall put the laver between the tabernacle of the congregation and the altar. And you shall put water there.

And you shall set up the court all around. And you shall place the hanging of the gate of the court.

And you shall take the oil of anointing, and you shall anoint the tabernacle and all in it. And you

shall sanctify it and all its vessels, and it shall become holy. (Exodus 40:1-9 LITV)

* * * * *

The Gates of the Kingdom

~

A story of seed-time and harvest, of sprouting and blossoming, of bearing fruit with seed unto the fullness ... A Kingdom sown, a Kingdom reaped, a glorious Bride without spot or wrinkle, a matchless gift from a Father to a Son; bone of His bone and flesh of His flesh.

Heritage Series

The Consummation

And it happened in the first month, (Abib) in the second year, on the first of the month, the tabernacle was raised up. And Moses finished all the work. (Exodus 40:17, 33b)

All that Oholi'av has spoken is true in every way. I, Avihu, son of Aharon, do not deny, but openly confess before you, my brother, my sister; we did not all enter into the work and the joy of Elohim in those days.

Those of us who frequented the tents of Zith' could see nothing of the glory of Y'haveh, nor did we go near the joy of the workers.

On the contrary, we drank to drown our sorrows. We could see that other people were happy. This actually made us feel worse.

I began to resent everyone's happiness. We ridiculed all the young men who wouldn't drink with us. In this we were greatly encouraged by our cousins from Uzi'el.

We respected no one when we were drinking, but demanded the respect of all our peers. We had seen Y'haveh. They had not. We were the sons of Aharon, and Elohim had called us by name.

Some of our elders were drinking too. They would say to us, 'Nadav, Avihu, 'ah, brothers, you should not drink so much. You are holy. Your father is Cohen. You should not be here.' But we never listened. They were drinking the same as us.

We never let Father find out how much we drank. Mother covered for us sometimes too, but she was really covering for his sake. I think he knew, but that catastrophe with the golden calf had affected Father a lot. He was not as strict as he once was. He seemed to have aged a great deal to us, and even slowed a bit in his manner. He never said anything to us, but we both knew what he would say if we put the issue in his face.

It is only by the grace of Y'haveh in our Saviour that I can make this confession today and tell our story through the Wind of Heaven, the Ruach Ha Kodesh. May his wind blow on you this day my friend for his presence is very, very real!

And you shall bring Aaron and his sons near the door of the Tabernacle of the Congregation, and you shall wash them with water.

And you shall clothe Aaron with holy garments. And you shall anoint him and sanctify him. And he shall minister as priest to Me.

And you shall bring near his sons. And you shall clothe them with tunics. And you shall anoint them, as you anointed their father. And they shall minister as priests to Me. And their anointing shall be for a perpetual priesthood for their generations.

And Moses did so, according to all Jehovah had commanded him, so he did. (Exodus 40:12-16 LITV)

It was during the fitting of our tunics that we, the sons of Aharon, began to get some idea of our high calling. Looking back today, I can see that in reality, we had no idea at all. In fact, we had completely the wrong idea. We thought we had been set apart to bring Elohim to the people!

How foolish we were! We didn't realize it at the time, but we were actually making Y'haveh Eloheinu, the creator of Heaven and Earth, a tool of our ministry! I feel so ashamed to make this confession to you. Praise him! His loving kindness, his grace and compassion; they endure to The Age!

This then is our story:

On the first day of Aviv, the first month of the second year, the Tabernacle was set up.

The cloud came down and covered it, and the glory of Y'haveh filled the Tabernacle. It was so glorious that even Moshe couldn't go in. Y'haveh would call to him from inside the tent, and Moshe would go and stand in the gate and listen.

I can't speak for anyone else, but certainly by this stage, Nadav and I had become infatuated with the glory of Y'haveh. It seems strange looking back now to see just how captivated we had become by the sh'khinah. His glory was all around us every day, and we didn't even see it.

To be honest, the only glory that we really had any inner experience of was the vainglory of the 'wine'! The more we drank, the more we wanted, and the more we wanted, the more we got. We 'gloried' in the 'wine' every night, and we had an insatiable hunger for glory. It was 'fool's gold'. We had no idea what real glory was, nor who it is! But we sure could see it. Everyone saw the sh'khinah[3].

---

3   The Sh'khinah was visibly breaking out from the pillar of cloud which glowed brightly at night.

It may sound to you like I'm making excuses, but that's just the way we were.

When at last the days of our consecration arrived, we were all highly motivated. We needed to be. The priesthood was hard work. It required a lot of discipline. We didn't know anything about a cross. We were violent men and we had a kingdom coming into view; 'a kingdom of priests; a holy nation.' From where we stood that sounded real good!

Come with me my brother, my sister, and together we shall go back through the gate and see those days of consecration and glory. These things you must see, for every seed has produced fruit after its own kind. This is why all the earth is full of the glory of Adonai! It has been even from the beginning!

Come! The gate has a latch. It is inside of you. If you know intuitively these things, then you have found the latch. Come! Come to the gate of the tabernacle, to the meeting ground of Isra'el, to the courtyard of Eloheinu…

There! Beside the old man! That's me! … Yeah; with the frizzy hair and stripy jacket. Nadav is the one to the right of Aharon, dressed in blue. My two little brothers, El'azar and Itamar are standing on my left.

What's happening? Well, you see those men carrying the screen? They're our cousins. That screen is going right around us because we're about to get washed and shaved. You might have noticed, all Isra'el is watching. The man speaking is Moshe …

"…and all of these things are what Y'haveh has commanded to be done."

Turning, Moses motions to Elkanah and Phinehus, the sons of Assir. Taking brass pitchers, they and their young cousins immediately depart the ranks of Levi, returning with water from the laver.

…we do not wish to be unclothed, but to be clothed. (2 Corinthians 5:4b)

Elkanah hands his pitcher to Moses. Holding it high above his head he pronounces the blessing, 'waiving' the water before the eyes of God. From the assembled host, the 'amen' carries with a power rarely heard from the ranks of Israel.

Five young Levites file in behind the screen and the washing begins.

Towels are flipped over the screen each time a hand appears, and standing basins are carried away and emptied. Linen shorts and singlet's follow the towels in much the same manner.

The screen files out with its bearers, and the whole host of Kohath assemble behind Aaron and his sons. Amminadab is in front, with Gershon to the right and Merari to the left, about twelve thousand men in all…

My friend, that was for me, the first time in ages I'd felt really clean. It was like all the failure of my past had been washed away. Just look at us! We stood there like we had nothing … dressed in only white shorts and singlets. There was nothing we could do. We could only stand and wait.

I remember having a very real sense that something more was happening than what we could see. We're all anticipating great heights. Now watch carefully. The cloaking is about to begin. The ministry of death shall be cloaked in garments of righteousness.

Here comes the tunic. It covers our flesh. Well, it tries to anyway, if you don't pay too much attention to what we do that is.

…Now the girdle; to cover our gluttony.

…And the upper robe so royal; to hide our low estate.

This is the ephod, it disguises our frailty. It says that the burden of the nation is upon the shoulders of the priesthood …And the girdle of the ephod to cloak our strivings as we struggle to earn the right to share in the exultation of Elohim. It doesn't work!

Yes! This piece is truly magnificent. It's the breastplate. On it are the twelve precious stones representing all the tribes. It hides our selfishness rather well don't you think?

Now you see what Moshe is doing? He's placing something into the breastplate. That's what we call the Urim and the Tumim; Lights and Perfections. They're there to make up for the darkness hidden by that turban. That darkness is a fearful thing, but that's just the way we were.

Finally, the golden plate, the holy crown upon the forehead of my earthly father is to remind everybody that Y'haveh has chosen to see us as holy; set apart for him!

Cloaked in these garments, it was not actually us he chose to see. He chose to see only the image of his son, with his tribal brothers. Bearing the twelve upon his heart and the kingdom upon his shoulders, he didn't try to exult himself, but rather, humbling himself, took the form of a servant. It was his glory and his honor that we put on, not our own. We wore the symbols of the one who is the glory and the honor of the Father.

For as many as were baptized into Christ, you put on Christ. (Galatians 3:27 LITV)

This is why everything was made and done according to his pattern. If only we had understood this then!

You ask how I know these things … I met him! We all shall meet him my friend. We all shall meet him! May your turn come not as mine, but with desire and fulfillment, with life and with glory! Amen!

You see that golden vessel Moshe is holding up before Adonai? It contains the holy anointing oil. It is unique. There is none like it anywhere. The fragrance of it always speaks of the holiness of Y'haveh. All the people know the fragrance. Can you smell it on the breeze? You soon shall…

Look! Moshe is anointing the dwelling place and everything in it. The whole tabernacle is permeated by the fragrance of holiness.

The altar is consecrated.

The oil is poured out on Aharon's head. It flows down on his beard even to his garments!

Behold! How good and how pleasant, the living of brothers, even in unity. It is like the precious oil on the head, that ran down on the beard; Aaron's beard; going down to the mouth of his garments; like the dew of Hermon coming down on the moun-

tains of Zion; for there Jehovah commanded the blessing: life till everlasting. (Psalm 133 LITV)

Now it's our turn. It's hard for you to imagine what we're feeling right now. Only brothers together could know. Look at those tunics, the red sashes and turbans. Moshe himself is crowning us. Our whole world has suddenly changed and we're standing in a new creation. It felt like we were moving into Heaven itself, but it was earth. The sun's still hot and we can feel the sand under our feet. I remember checking … Just to make sure.

To confess the truth; we felt like Ben Elohim. It's just a picture, but we are the picture, and that day we could sense the reality. Somehow it's there!

"My decree is: 'You are elohim, sons of the Most High all of you. Nevertheless, you will die like mortals; like any prince, you will fall.'" (Psalm 82:6-7 CJB)

…The commotion in the crowd behind us? Oh! That'll be Uri; B'tzal'el's father. He's bringing the sin offering. Those are all his sons following behind with the bull. We always use two ropes on a bull when there's a crowd.

B'tzal'el is the one coming last. He's always been frightened of bulls.

Me 'n Nadav, we're not usually frightened of bulls, but this bull was different.

You see the five of us laying hands on its head? Well, we are placing all that we represent into that bull. Look! Nadav cuts the throat. Everything comes gushing out. I know! I hold the basin. See!

It was not until I met him that I discovered what Heaven's eyes could see in that blood. The poured out life of Yeshua Ha Mashiach was seen by Y'haveh my true 'av in that blood! We could only see ourselves, and our penalty paid. It made me tremble.

There will be three sacrifices today, this bull and two rams. Come with me beyond this equinox to the cool of the evening, to the ram of our consecrations and the fellowship meal of lamb…

And he brought the second ram, a ram of the consecrations, and Aaron and his sons lay their hands on the head of the ram. And one killed it, and Moses took of its blood and put it on the tip of the right ear of Aaron, and on the thumb of his right hand, and on the big toe of his right foot.

And he brought Aaron's sons, and Moses put of the blood on the tip of their right ear, and on the thumb of their right hand, and on the big toe of their right foot. And Moses sprinkled the blood on the altar all around… (Leviticus 8:22-24 LITV)

Then, a symbol of the offerings, and of our service toward Y'haveh, was caused to pass through our hands. This, every day for seven days, and still we did not understand.

...And Moses took the breast and waved it, a wave offering before Jehovah, of the ram of the consecrations. It was Moses' portion, as Jehovah had commanded Moses.

And Moses took of the anointing oil, and of the blood on the altar, and sprinkled on Aaron, on his garments, and on his sons and the garments of his sons with him... (Leviticus 8:29-30 LITV)

"Boil the flesh in the gate of the Tabernacle!"

"'Ahi, you and your ben shall eat it there, along with the bread which is left in the basket of consecrations. If anything remains, burn it!"

"Neither you nor your ben shall leave the gate of the Tent for seven days, until the days of your consecration are fulfilled. Y'haveh shall consecrate you seven days."

"Just as he has done today, so also shall be done for seven days! You shall remain in the gate day and night for seven days. This is so that you will know to keep the charge of Y'haveh and you will not die, for so I have been commanded!"

My friend: that command came as a great shock to me. I think 'Av knew, but it sure rocked me 'n Nadav. At that time, we just couldn't imagine what it'd be like to go seven whole days without a drink.

We counted the days. We should have also counted the nights!

At the end of the seventh day, after the fellowship meal of lamb, when everything was quiet, we went back to camp; straight to the tents of Zith.

Sometime before dawn we stumbled into dreamland.

*And it happened, on the eighth day, Moses **called** for Aaron and for his sons, and for the elders of Israel. (Leviticus 9:1 LITV)*

"Avihu! Nadav! Wake up! Wake up!"

It was only mother. I rolled over and went back to sleep...

"Get up! Whack!" A broom handle across the rib cage: It was Auntie Miryam! We both crawled to our feet.

"OK! OK! We're up."

"Don't talk to me in that manner of voice you young rebel! Now get dressed and get over to the tent quick smart or I'll be making trouble for the both of you! And sober up! You might be Cohen[4] now but I'm still your doda! You think you're so special but all I see is a couple of young drunks! And don't either of you go thinking you can get away with anything around here on account of those new clothes!"

"We've been ordained," replied Nadav rather sheepishly. Boy, he sure must have been drunk to talk back to Auntie Miryam.

"Vainglory is fools' gold young man! Worse than that, it'll do nothing but land you in trouble and all of us along with you! And as for being Cohen, the man is Cohen who performs priestly function. This is your first day as Cohen so you'd better start acting like Cohen …both of you!"

As we approached the gate, Nadav was still venting his frustration at Auntie.

"Can't she see that we've come up in the world? For seven days we've been the center of all Isra'el. And she still treats us like children! What'll it take for them to see? In the very gate of Yisra'el, have we not gained rights that set us above all our 'ah!?"

"Today we shall be like Aharon and even like Moshe himself and all the people will bow down. Just do what I do little 'ah, you'll see. It'll happen!"

---

4   Cohen: Priests

It sounded good to me as we walked along arm in arm. That was the only way we could walk a straight line. We didn't want anyone to notice that we'd been drinking. Nadav gave the last half-skin to our cousins along the way with strict instructions not to drink it.

Since we had done most of the work the previous evening, it was more or less expected that El'azar and Itamar would serve first that day.

Even so, I almost tripped carrying the blood of the sin offering that was for us and Father.

I held up the basin to Father, and as he dipped his finger into the blood, he looked into my eyes. I detected only the slightest frown, but it felt like he could see right through me. He knew, and I knew he knew.

He carried on without wavering. Phfewh! 'Saved' by the expectation of ceremony!

He smeared the blood on each horn of the altar and poured out the rest at its base. The fat, the kidneys and the fold of the liver, Nadav brought to him and he burned it with incense on the altar.

It was a relief to carry the flesh and the skin out to our cousins who burned it beyond the camp. There was a great pile of sintered bone fragments and charcoal. I distinctly remember a chill running up my spine as I looked at it. Had no idea, of course, why! This was the chance for us to gulp a swig or two while no-one was watching.

Coming back to the gate, it really struck me that all of Isra'el was assembled. The witnesses to our actions were without number. There was tremendous pressure. Even so, it was not the great cloud of witnesses that we feared, but Moshe!

We slaughtered the calf and the lamb of the burnt offering, ('ola) prepared them and made them to go up in smoke ('ola) upon the altar.

We also offered up the goat of the sin offering, the food offering, and the peace offering. Well, although we did the work, it wasn't really us who offered it, but Father and he not for himself, but for all the people.

Moshe was watching all of this very closely from his seat in the gate. Nadav was performing his duties with unusual vigor. I was sure that Moshe would notice something was wrong.

When I tried to signal him to slow down, he stopped dead and looked at me! Oh, no! I looked the other way, and out of the corner of my eye, noticed that maybe Moshe hadn't seen it. Y'hoshua was speaking in his ear and he'd turned his head for a moment. I wondered what Y'hoshua was saying. Was he speaking about us? ...I didn't know.

Father was waiting for us up on the platform beside the altar. As we went up, I put my arm behind Nadav to steady him.

We took the fat of the peace offering from the breasts where we'd placed it earlier, and Father made it to be ʿola upon the altar.

When we turned to go down, there was Moshe, waiting for us!

I was terrified. Nadav didn't even seem to notice. He went straight to his place beside Itamar. I kept my eyes on my feet going down the steps. When I looked up, Moshe was right in front of me. He looked into my eyes for but a moment. I felt like I'd been hit by lightning!

Father raised up the waive offering before Y'haveh, one piece at a time. All eyes shifted there, especially those of us priests who would eat it.

So you see, I had escaped again, but somehow I knew the escape would be short-lived. I knew something was terribly wrong, but I couldn't see what it was because it was inside of me.

And Aaron lifted up his hands toward the people and blessed them, and came down from offering the sin offering, and the burnt offering, and the peace offerings.

And Moses and Aaron went into the tabernacle of the congregation. And they came out and blessed the people, and the glory of Jehovah appeared to all the people.

And fire came out from before Jehovah and consumed the burnt offering, and the fat on the altar. And all the people saw, and cried aloud, and fell on their faces.

It was like a signal had been given to Nadav. As soon as he saw the people fall on their faces, he went into action. We both did!

Quickly, and with great zeal, we each took our own fire-pan, put fire and incense in them, and rushed into the tent where Moshe and Aharon had just been. Now it was our turn! We would make fire come out from Y'haveh, and all the people would bow down!

Moshe and Father both saw us, turned, and looked questioningly to each other as we rushed past them. There before us was that small golden altar. Incense was wafting up from it. We went straight to it and placed our fire there. We stepped back and bowed down. I glanced across at Nadav and he at me. We each had a gleam in our eye.

We waited a few moments, and rose up to go out and receive our applause.

As we approached the entrance of the tent, we raised our hands and "WHOOFF!!!" Fire!!!! On us!!!!! Nadav was a ball of flame! He crumbled and so did I! The pain was intense. Screaming, we writhed in the dust for endless moments senselessly clawing at our pain. Everything went dark; dark and smoky!

I remembered the pile of bones and ashes, as I drifted off, 'ola, from what I had become. The darkness was very, very deep. It was bottomless.

....

For you have not come to a tangible mountain, to an ignited fire, to darkness, to murk, to a whirlwind, to the sound of a shofar, and to a voice whose words made the hearers beg that no further message be given to them – for they couldn't bear what was being commanded them, "If even an animal touches the mountain, it is to be stoned to death"; and so terrifying was the sight that Moshe said, "I am quaking with dread."

On the contrary, you have come to mount Tziyon, that is, the city of the living God, heavenly Yerushalayim; to myriads of angels in festive assembly; to a Judge who is God of everyone; to spirits of righteous people who have been brought to the goal; to the mediator of a new covenant, Yesh-

ua; and to the sprinkled blood that speaks better things than the blood of Hevel.

See that you don't reject the One speaking! For if those did not escape who rejected him when he gave divine warning on earth, think how much less we will escape if we turn away from Him who warns from heaven. Even then, His voice shook the earth; but now, He has made this promise:

"One more time I will shake not only the earth, but heaven too!"

And this phrase, "one more time", makes clear that the things shaken are removed, since they are created things, so that the things not shaken may remain. Therefore, since we have received an unshakable Kingdom, let us have grace, through which we may offer service that will please God, with reverence and fear. For indeed, "Our God is a consuming fire!" (Hebrews 12:18-29 CJB)

"'...We consider the arrogant happy; also evildoers prosper; they put God to the test; nevertheless, they escape.'"

Then those who feared Adonai spoke together; and Adonai listened and heard.

A record book was written in his presence for those who feared Adonai and had respect for his name.

"They will be mine," says Adonai-Tzva'ot, *(the Lord of Heaven's Armies)* "on the day when I compose my own special treasure. I will spare them as a man spares his own son who serves him. Then once again you will see the difference between the righteous and the wicked, between the person who serves God and the one that doesn't serve him. For the day is coming, burning like a furnace, when all the proud and evil doers will be stubble; the day that is coming will set them ablaze," says Adonai-Tzva'ot, "and leave them neither root nor branch."

"But to you who fear my name, the sun of righteousness will rise with healing in its wings; and you will break out leaping, like calves released from the stall. You will trample the wicked, they will be ashes under the soles of your feet on the day when I take action," says Adonai-Tzva'ot.

"Remember the Torah of Moshe my servant, which I enjoined on him at Horev..." *(Malachi 3:15-4:4a CJB)* *(...symbolized by the burning thorn-bush, which was not consumed.)*

On every High Mountain and lofty hill will be streams and flowing brooks, on a day of great slaughter, when the towers fall. Moreover, the light of the moon will be as bright as the light of the sun; and the light of the sun will be seven times stronger, like the light of seven days (in one), on *the day Adonai binds up the wounds of his people and heals the bruise caused by the blow. (Isaiah 30:25-26 CJB)*

"When the day of the harvest of Avihu is fully come, I will take action, and I will remove the sin of this land in a single day," says Adonai-Tzva'ot!

And Moses said to Aaron, It is that which Jehovah has spoken, saying, I will be sanctified by those drawing near to Me; and I will be honored before all the people. And Aaron was silent.

And Moses called Mishael and Elzaphan, sons of Uzziel, Aaron's uncle, and said to them, Come near, carry your brothers from the front of the sanctuary to the outside of the camp. And they came near and carried them in their coats to the outside of the camp.

. . . .

Epilogue

I trembled as I sensed my consciousness returning. The darkness receded, and a great light was approaching. I heard him call my name … again; as on the mountain. There was warmth and comfort in his voice. I responded. I followed him.

I thought that I was dreaming in a land where there was no dreaming.

When I opened my eyes, I realized that I …my spirit that is, was actually in motion! I was carried by a swift and irresistible power towards the light above the pavement I had seen on the mountain, and to the foot of the throne of our God.

And seated upon the throne was One like a son of man. His feet were like glowing metal fired in a furnace. His eyes were like blazing fire. The hair of his head was brilliant white, like wool.

There is no creature unrevealed before him; but all things are naked and laid bare to his eyes.

I knew my sin. My flesh was consumed, but my inner being was naked before him. I fell prostrate at his feet and wept.

Then he spoke …his voice; the same that had called my name …It was regal beyond description. 'This one is mine,' he said, 'put clean garments on him and give him a place amongst those who witness the way of my cross. He is one who has not yet known it.'

'He is Ben Ya'akov. I have chosen that he shall be Ben Yisra'el. He is mine and precious in my eyes.'

So you see my brother, my sister, it is by his grace that I've been saved for, by his grace, I was allowed to witness grace. Grace upon grace. The fire consumed my flesh, but grace alone has consumed me.

The Avihu of Misrayim and Sinai is no more; consumed, not by fire, but by the passion of a cross that consumes all things, a cross I had never known. Never again shall I glory except in the cross of Yeshua Ha Mashiach, my Lord and my Savior.

My hunger is for the cross in which I bow my will to the will of my father. It is only in his glory, that I shall ever now glory.

The source of the river of life is found in sharing in that glory alone. There is no other source of true life. All else is but an image, a picture, or as with vainglory; a mutation of what is real.

My brother, my sister, desire the cross. Look for his way. Let your hunger and your thirst chase no other glory and the Lord of Glory will be with your spirit.

Amen!

●●●●●●●●●●●●

Now if that which worked death, by means of a written text engraved on stone tablets, came with glory – such glory that the people of Isra'el could not stand to look at Moshe's face because of it's brightness, even though that brightness was al-

ready fading away – wont the working of the Spirit be accompanied with even greater glory? For if there was glory in what worked to declare people guilty, how much more must the glory abound in what works to declare people innocent! (2 Corinthians 3:7-9 JNT)

Shalom!

www.colininthespirit.com

Other Copyright

❋ ❋ ❋ ❋ ❋

Other Books by Colin Baker

from The Voice Series:

The Voice in Galatians

The Voice in Thessalonians

The Voice in 1 Corinthians

...with more to come.

from The Gates of the Kingdom Series:

The Gates of the Kingdom Part 1

The Gates of the Kingdom Part 3

The Little Gate of the Great King

...with more to come.

These titles and many more are available in PDF, ePub and Audio format for Laptop, Tablet and Mobile devices from
www.colininthespirit.com

❈ ❈ ❈ ❈ ❈

About the Author

Colin Baker lives in Australia's Northern Territory in the remote Aboriginal Homeland Community of Gäwa.

Gäwa is a name well loved. It's origins are Macassan. It means 'Land of the King'.

His experience at Gäwa has been one of pioneering and gate-keeping, perseverance, patience and overcoming.

He is committed to the glory of God as is reflected in his vision to facilitate an embracing of the Gospel of the Glory by God's people.

His mandate is pictured in Ezekiel chapter one when viewed in the light of the fact that 'movement in the Spiritual Realm is by vision'. ...And that the Lord's Community is the vehicle that transports the throne and the One seated upon it into all the Earth.

www.ingramcontent.com/pod-product-compliance
Lightning Source LLC
Chambersburg PA
CBHW070525030426
42337CB00016B/2113